ANCIENT GREECE

by Catherine C. Finan

BEARPORT
PUBLISHING

Minneapolis, Minnesota

Credits:

Title page, 10 top, Philipp von Foltz/Public Domain; 4 top, Anastasios71/Shutterstock; 4 right, Georgios Alexandris/Shutterstock; 4 left, Rainer Lesniewski/Shutterstock; 5 top, frantic00/Shutterstock.com; 5 middle, 13 bottom, 14 left, 15 top left, 15 bottom, 17 middle, 18 middle, 21 bottom, 23 top middle, 24 bottom, 25 bottom, 27 top left, Public Domain; 5 bottom, kostasgr/Shutterstock; 5 bottom left, Ljupco Smokovski/Shutterstock; 5 bottom right, Massimo Todaro/Shutterstock.com; 6, Georgios Tsichlis/Shutterstock; 6 left, Daniel Eskridge/Shutterstock; 6 middle, Fyodor Bronnikov/Public Domain; 6 right, Anatoliy Karlyuk/Shutterstock; 7 top, Leo von Klenze/Public Domain; 7 top middle, Fotokvadrat/Shutterstock; 7 left, ArtFamily/Shutterstock; 7 right, Littlekidmoment/Shutterstock; 8 top, Joseph Gandy/Public Domain; 8 left, Oleg Senkov/Shutterstock.com; 8 middle, Noppadon stocker/Shutterstock; 8 right, FREEPIK2/Shutterstock; 9 top, lornet/Shutterstock.com; 9 top left, 9 bottom right, 13 bottom center, Massimo Todaro/Shutterstock.com; 9 top right, George E. Koronaios/Creative Commons; 9 bottom, Firstear/Shutterstock; 10 bottom, Creative Commons; 11 top, sirtravelalot/Shutterstock; 11 bottom trabantos/Shutterstock; 11 bottom left, 11 middle right, Anne-Louis Girodet de Roussy-Trioson/Public Domain; 11 bottom right, 11 bottom middle left, Bénigne Gagneraux/Public Domain; 11 bottom middle, Roman Samborskyi/Shutterstock; 12 top, Nina Alizada/Shutterstock; 12 left, 19 bottom right, Gelpi/Shutterstock; 12 right, Lawrence Alma-Tadema/Public Domain; 12 middle, MSPhotographic/Shutterstock; 13 top left, 19 bottom middle, 22 bottom, LightField Studios/Shutterstock; 13 top, matrioshka/Shutterstock; 13 bottom of top image, 17 top, Jacob von Falke/Public Domain; 13 bottom right, In Green/Shutterstock; 14 bottom, Georgios Kritsotakis/Shutterstock.com; 14 right, Olga Evans/Shutterstock; 15 top, Anton Chygarev/Shutterstock; 15 top right, Elena11/Shutterstock; 15 bottom right, Syda Productions/Shutterstock; 16 top, Raphael/Public Domain; 16 bottom left, Henryk Siemiradzki/Public Domain; 16 bottom right, 17 bottom left, John William Waterhouse/Public Domain; 17 top left, Jeka/Shutterstock; 17 right, ojellavm/Shutterstock; 18 top, Mark and Anna Photography/Shutterstock; 18 top right, Caroline Lena Becker/Creative Commons; 18 bottom, Dmitry Chulov/ Shutterstock.com; 18 top, latino/Shutterstock; 18 top left, Anders Peter Photography/Shutterstock; 18 top right, le bouil baptiste/Shutterstock; 19 bottom left, Marcin-linfernum/Shutterstock; 19 bottom middle left, Aviad Bublil/Creative Commons; 20 top, Leo von Klenze/Public Domain; 20 middle, Sven Hansche/Shutterstock; 20 bottom, kostasgr/Shutterstock; 21 top, Rob Crandall/ Shutterstock.com; 21 top right, Prostock-studio/Shutterstock; 21 bottom left, Kamira/Shutterstock; 21 bottom right, Tymonko Galyna/Shutterstock; 22 top, carlos corzo/Creative Commons; 22 top right, Kues/Shutterstock; 22 bottom right, Roman Samborskyi/Shutterstock; 23 top, Dave & Margie Hill/Kleerup/Public Domain; 23 bottom, Constantine Pan/Shutterstock; 23 bottom left, Juice Flair/Shutterstock; 23 bottom right, Gilmanshin/Shutterstock; 24 top, S-F/Shutterstock; 24 top middle, Daniel Eskridge/Shutterstock; 25 top, dtopal/Shutterstock; 26, Morphart Creation/Shutterstock; 26 Jihan Nafiaa Zahri/Shutterstock; 27 top right, myboys.me/Shutterstock; 27 top center, I, Mogi/Creative Commons; 27 bottom, New Africa/Shutterstock; 27 bottom left, Fyodor Bronnikov/Public Domain; 27 bottom right, Nanette Dreyer/Shutterstock; 28 top left, Gift of Benedict XIV, 1748/Public Domain; 28 top right, Giovanni Dall'Orto/Creative Commons; 28 bottom, Albani Collection, then in the Musei Capitolini; seized during the French Revolution then exchanged according to the Tolentino Treaty, 1815/Public Domain; 28 bottom right, 28-29, Auster Photography

President: Jen Jenson
Director of Product Development: Spencer Brinker
Senior Editor: Allison Juda
Associate Editor: Charly Haley
Designer: Colin O'Dea

Developed and produced for Bearport Publishing by BlueAppleWorks Inc.
Managing Editor for BlueAppleWorks: Melissa McClellan
Art Director: T.J. Choleva
Photo Research: Jane Reid

Library of Congress Cataloging-in-Publication Data

Names: Finan, Catherine C., 1972- author.
Title: Ancient Greece / Catherine C. Finan.
Description: Minneapolis, Minnesota : Bearport Publishing Company, [2022] | Series: X-treme facts: ancient history | Includes bibliographical references and index.
Identifiers: LCCN 2021001072 (print) | LCCN 2021001073 (ebook) | ISBN 9781636910932 (library binding) | ISBN 9781636911007 (paperback) | ISBN 9781636911076 (ebook)
Subjects: LCSH: Greece--Civilization--To 146 B.C.--Miscellanea--Juvenile literature.
Classification: LCC DF77 .F496 2022 (print) | LCC DF77 (ebook) | DDC 938--dc23
LC record available at https://lccn.loc.gov/2021001072
LC ebook record available at https://lccn.loc.gov/2021001073

For more information, write to Bearport Publishing, 5357 Penn Avenue South, Minneapolis, MN 55419. Printed in the United States of America

Contents

Amazing Ancient Greece 4

A Civilization Is Born 6

Don't Mess with Sparta 8

The Dawn of Democracy 10

At Home with the Ancient Greeks 12

Dressing the Part 14

Growing Up Greek 16

Gods and Goddesses of Mount Olympus 18

Built for the Gods 20

Take Me to the Theater 22

Olympic Origins 24

Ancient Greece Lives On 26

Theater Mask 28

Glossary 30

Read More 31

Learn More Online 31

Index 32

About the Author 32

Amazing Ancient Greece

Beep, beep, beep! It's time to wake up! Before you hit snooze, did you know your alarm clock was invented by the ancient Greeks? And that's not all. They also invented a little thing called **democracy**! With their work in math, science, art, technology, and even sports, we can thank the ancient Greeks for helping to create our modern world. Let's head to ancient Greece to learn more about this amazing civilization!

Many remains of ancient Greece still stand today.

FATHER OF MEDICINE? AWW . . . I WAS JUST DOING MY JOB.

ATLANTIC OCEAN

EUROPE

BLACK SEA

MEDITERRANEAN SEA

Greece

AFRICA

Ancient Greek **physician Hippocrates** is often called the father of medicine.

Today's stadiums and theaters are modeled after the ones built in ancient Greece.

IT REALLY DOES LOOK LIKE A MODERN STADIUM.

YEAH, BUT WHERE ARE THE SNACK STANDS?

Several of ancient Greece's theaters are still used today for concerts and other performances.

The Greek mathematician Eratosthenes figured out the distance around Earth more than 2,200 years ago!

COME ON, MAN! PICK UP THE PACE!

YOU TRY DOING THIS IN SANDALS!

The marathon was born when an ancient Greek messenger ran 25 miles (40 km) from Marathon to Athens.

A Civilization Is Born

Ancient Greek civilization didn't just pop up overnight. It developed over hundreds of years from two earlier civilizations: the Minoan (mih-NOH-in) on the island of Crete and the Mycenaean (my-sih-NAY-in) on the Greek mainland. Greek city-states, made up of powerful cities and their surrounding areas, began to form around 800 BCE. But there was one big problem—they just couldn't get along!

The Minoan civilization was named for a **mythological** king who kept a **pet monster under the city. It had a bull's head and a man's body!** Yikes!

I DON'T WANT TO GO BACK INSIDE YET!

BE A GOOD BOY AND I'LL GIVE YOU A TREAT!

HE SHOULD HAVE JUST GOTTEN A DOG.

The ancient Greeks didn't consider themselves Greek! They were citizens of their city-states. And they would fight about it, too!

The act of shaking hands to greet someone goes back as far as ancient Greece!

The Mycenaeans were the first to speak Greek and are often called the first Greeks.

Don't Mess with Sparta

The biggest ancient Greek city-state **rivalry** was between Athens and Sparta. They fought a series of long, bloody battles known as the Peloponnesian War. Why all the fussing and fighting? Well, Athens had grown into a wealthy trading empire. Sparta was jealous. After a spat over the city-state Corinth, Sparta declared war on Athens. In the end, Sparta—with its famously fierce soldiers—won the war.

The people of Sparta believed they were directly related to Hercules, the famous Greek hero!

WHAT DO YOU WANT, KID? I'M BUSY HERE!

I THOUGHT YOU MIGHT WANT TO BORROW SOME CLOTHES.

Unlike other Greek city-states, Sparta let young girls learn wrestling and other sports.

PACK YOUR THINGS. YOU'RE IN THE ARMY NOW!

WHAT DOES HE WANT?

US!

NO MORE FUN FOR YOU.

At age seven, Spartan boys left home to begin military training.

I'VE HEARD YOU'RE GOING TO RETIRE SOON.

WHAT? NO WAY! I'M ONLY 45!

Spartan soldiers didn't retire until they were 60 years old!

The red color of a soldier's **tunic** was meant to hide bloody battle wounds. *Ew!*

The Dawn of Democracy

Not all power in ancient Greece was in the hands of the military. Ordinary people had power, too. This was thanks to the Greek invention of democracy, which developed about 2,500 years ago in Athens. Men of the city-state took part in government, served on **juries**, and voted on important matters. This was a *huge* change from the past, when just a few wealthy landowners controlled life in the city-states.

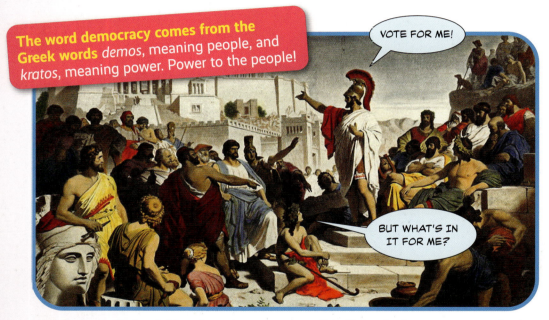

The word democracy comes from the Greek words *demos*, meaning people, and *kratos*, meaning power. Power to the people!

VOTE FOR ME!

BUT WHAT'S IN IT FOR ME?

Unfortunately, Athenian democracy didn't include everyone. Only men over the age of 18 who were born in Athens could vote.

The Pnyx was a hill in central Athens where citizens met to debate and vote.

Ancient Greeks were the first to use jury trials to decide if people broke the law. Now, it's part of the U.S. Constitution!

At Home with the Ancient Greeks

The work of ancient Greek democracy happened in public spaces. But daily life was centered in the home. Most ancient Greek homes had stone floors, tile roofs, and walls made of mud and brick. Typical homes were small, with a few rooms built around a courtyard. There, families gathered to eat and relax. Homes were lit with candles and oil lamps, so when it got too dark, it was bedtime!

Most homes didn't have bathrooms. Many people used public bathrooms whenever they had to go.

Instead of toilet paper, ancient Greeks cleaned themselves with small stones! Ouch!

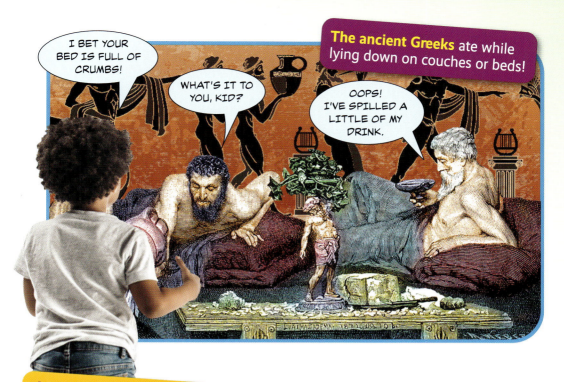

The ancient Greeks ate while lying down on couches or beds!

I BET YOUR BED IS FULL OF CRUMBS!

WHAT'S IT TO YOU, KID?

OOPS! I'VE SPILLED A LITTLE OF MY DRINK.

Ancient Greek beds were sometimes stuffed with dry grass, feathers, or wool.

WELL, STUFF IT YOURSELF NEXT TIME!

THIS BED IS VERY PRICKLY AND ITCHY!

Dressing the Part

Now that we're in an ancient Greek home, let's take a look in the closet! No matter where you'd look in ancient Greece, you'd see the same outfits. Belted tunics were all the rage. Over that, the Greeks would wear cloaks. People usually went barefoot, but leather sandals were often the hottest footwear fashion. Wearing jewelry made of gold and silver was another way to stand out from the crowd.

Clothing was often white, but the wealthy sometimes wore **bright clothing dyed with plants or even insects!**

A WHITE TUNIC IS JUST ANCIENT HISTORY!

WRONG! WHITE IS ALWAYS A CLASSIC.

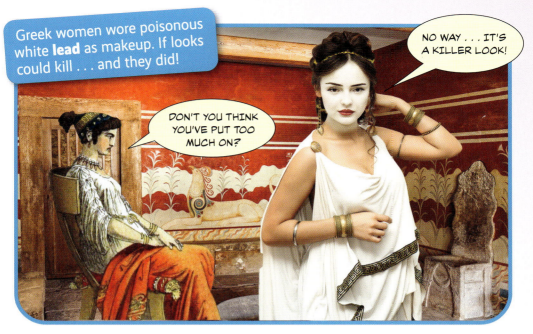

Women wore their long hair in curls, braids, and headbands.

Men styled their short hair with perfumes and oils.

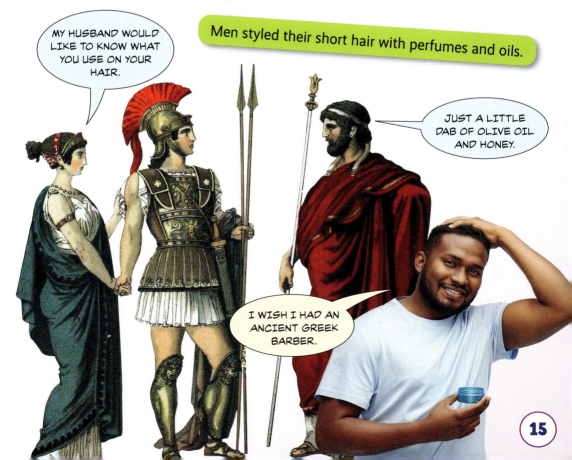

Growing Up Greek

The ancient Greek alarm clock has rung. The tunic is on. And the crumby breakfast in bed is over. What's an ancient Greek kid to do all day? Younger Greek children spent a lot of time with their mothers. Then, when they were old enough, it was time to learn! But in most of ancient Greece, schooling was *very* different for boys and girls.

Wealthy Greek boys went to school to learn science, math, **literature**, politics, music, and art.

TAKE THIS AND MEMORIZE PAGES 14 TO 36 FOR YOUR NEXT EXAM.

The best students often ended up studying at Plato's Academy, a famous school in Athens.

BUT I WANTED TO PLAY PIG BALL THIS WEEK!

Students had to memorize and recite very long poems!

For fun, children often **played with balls made from inflated pigs bladders.** Gross!

WHERE ARE ALL THE BOYS?

OUT THERE, PLAYING WITH THAT SMELLY BALL AGAIN.

Greek girls stayed home and learned how to cook, weave, and run a household.

Greek children played with yo-yos at least 2,500 years ago!

I WANT TO PLAY, TOO!

WHAT A SHOW-OFF!

THANKS FOR THE BEST TOY EVER, GUYS!

YOU CAN PLAY AFTER YOUR COOKING CLASS.

Gods and Goddesses of Mount Olympus

In ancient Greece, children were taught that gods and goddesses controlled *everything*—from the weather, to how crops grew, to a battle's outcome. The gods were said to live on Mount Olympus, Greece's tallest mountain. They looked and acted like humans but also had superpowers. To keep their gods happy and calm, Greeks **worshipped** them at home and at temples. Angry Greek gods were no joke!

Zeus was the king of the Greek gods. He controlled the weather and could throw lightning bolts!

The warrior goddess Athena was born—already dressed in full armor—from Zeus's head!

The half-god Perseus killed the monstrous **Medusa, who had snakes for hair!**

Poseidon caused earthquakes by striking the ground with his trident.

Built for the Gods

Gods and goddesses didn't just control the lives of ancient Greeks—they inspired their art and **architecture**, too. Temples featured tall **columns** that rose up to the skies. Sculptures and pottery were filled with scenes featuring gods and other figures from Greek mythology. And the art and architecture of ancient Greece was so impressive that it has been copied in places all over the world for thousands of years—including the United States!

YEAH, I WAS KIND OF A BIG DEAL.

The Parthenon, Greece's most famous temple, was built to honor the goddess Athena.

Millions of tourists visit the ruins of the Parthenon in Athens every year.

Many ancient Greek temples and sculptures are now white, but most used to be painted bright colors!

The Supreme Court Building in Washington, D.C. was built **to look similar to the Parthenon!**

WOW! THIS IS AS GREEK AS IT GETS!

The Supreme Court Building is held up by tall Corinthian columns.

There are three styles of ancient Greek columns. Doric columns have plain tops. Ionic columns have scroll-shaped tops. Corinthian columns have the fanciest tops!

I FEEL SO FANCY!

Doric

Ionic

Corinthian

Even the most decorated painted pottery still had everyday uses like carrying and storing water.

LOOK AT THAT BEAUTIFUL POTTERY!

YUP, WE NEED TO STEP UP OUR GAME!

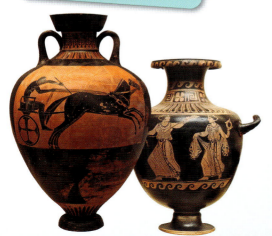

Take Me to the Theater

Ancient Greeks didn't just go big with their temples—their theaters were large, too! Rows of seats for thousands of people surrounded the stage in a semicircle. And the shows were just as spectacular as the locations where they were performed. Plays often had live music, and many even had special effects! The Greek stages might remind you of our own theaters and stadiums. Yep, we got these ideas from the Greeks as well!

Theaters in ancient Greece were open-air, meaning there wasn't a roof over your head if it started to rain.

DONT FORGET YOUR UMBRELLA!

WHAT A CRUEL WORLD!

OH, LIGHTEN UP ALREADY!

Actors wore masks with big frowns in **tragedies** and big smiles in **comedies**.

I'LL NEED SOME WOMEN'S CLOTHES TO GO WITH THIS MASK!

Ancient Greek actors were always men. They played both male and female characters.

Greek actors playing gods appeared to fly with the help of cranes. Special machines made thunder sounds!

One story says the famous **Greek playwright Sophocles died from lack of breath after reciting** a long line from one of his plays!

MR. SOPHOCLES, CAN WE DO A SELFIE?

OKAY, BUT DO IT QUICKLY. I'M DYING HERE!

Olympic Origins

The ancient Greeks didn't just love plays. They loved sports, too! In fact, we can thank them for the biggest sports **competition** we have today—the Olympics! The first Olympic Games were held in 776 BCE to honor Zeus. Ancient Olympic events included running, wrestling, **chariot** racing, boxing, and **javelin** throwing. The Olympics were so important that warring city-states stopped their battles to peacefully take part in the Games!

The first Games were held in Olympia and named for Mount Olympus.

DON'T MAKE ME COME DOWN THERE!

NO FIGHTING DURING THE GAMES!

NO PROBLEM, I'LL GET YOU LATER!

Only Greek men could take part in the Games.

Women had their own athletic competition, called Heraia. It honored the goddess Hera.

The original Olympic athletes competed completely naked!

There were only two rules in the mixed martial arts–style sport known as pankration: no biting and no **gouging**!

There were no medals awarded at the ancient Olympics. The winners were given wreaths of olive branches instead.

Ancient Greece Lives On

Around 146 BCE, Greece was taken over by the Romans who went on to develop a civilization that borrowed heavily from Greek culture. In modern times, we also owe much to the ancient Greeks. We can thank the Greeks for how we govern, how we live, and how we play! The influences of the ancient Greeks remain all around us.

Mathematician Archimedes invented the first **odometer**.

The word alphabet comes from the first two Greek letters—*alpha* and *beta*.

The ancient Greek computer was used to count days and months to keep their calendars accurate.

Theater Mask
Craft Project

Actors in Greek theater wore masks with big smiles and frowns while performing. The extreme facial expressions could be seen from a distance. And actors could play more than one role using different masks. The actors changed masks out of sight so the audience wouldn't see. Then, they started acting as a whole new character.

Theater masks from ancient Greece are displayed in museums all over the world.

What You Will Need

- A pencil
- A paper plate
- Scissors
- Masking tape
- Markers
- A craft stick
- Construction paper
- Craft glue

Step One

Use a pencil to draw a happy or sad face on the back of a paper plate.

Step Two

Use scissors to cut out the eyes and mouth that you drew on the paper plate.

Step Three

Tape a craft stick to the back of the paper plate to make a handle.

Step Four

Decorate the front of the mask. Draw a nose. Outline the mouth and eyes with markers. Cut hair from construction paper and glue to the mask.

Glossary

architecture a style or method of building

chariot a carriage with two wheels that is pulled by horses

columns tall upright pillars that help support a building

comedies plays that are funny or happy

competition a contest or game

democracy a form of government in which people choose leaders by voting

gouging scratching or cutting a deep hole or gash

javelin a long spear that people throw as far as they can as a sport

juries groups of people that listen to facts at trials and make decisions about who is to blame

lead a soft metal that is harmful if ingested

literature written works, such as poems, plays, and books

mythological relating to a set of stories, folklore, or beliefs of a particular group or culture

odometer a tool that measures the distance traveled by a vehicle

physician a doctor of medicine

tragedies plays with unhappy endings

tunic a loose shirt that usually hangs to the knees

worshipped honored and respected as a god

Read More

Bell, Samantha S., and Adrienne Beaucage. *Ancient Greece (Ancient Civilizations).* New York: AV2, 2021.

Flynn, Sarah Wassner. *Greek Mythology (Weird but True! Know it All).* Washington, D.C.: National Geographic, 2018.

Green, Sara. *Ancient Greece (Blastoff! Discovery: Ancient Civilizations).* Minneapolis: Bellwether Media, 2020.

Learn More Online

1. Go to **www.factsurfer.com**

2. Enter "**Ancient Greece**" into the search box.

3. Click on the cover of this book to see a list of websites.

Index

architecture 20

art 4, 16, 20

Athena 18, 20

Athens 5, 8, 10–11, 16, 20

city-states 6–8, 10, 24

clothing 14, 23

columns 20–21

democracy 4, 10, 12

gods 18–20, 23–24

home 6, 9, 12, 14, 16–18

juries 10–11

Minoan 6

Mount Olympus 18, 24

Mycenaeans 6–7

mythology 6, 20

Olympics 24–25

pottery 20–21, 25

Romans 26

school 16

sculptures 20

Sparta 8–9

temples 18, 20, 22

theaters 5, 22, 28

Zeus 18–19

About the Author

Catherine C. Finan is a writer living in northeastern Pennsylvania. She enjoys writing about a wide range of subjects, including ancient history, and is a bit obsessed with Greek mythology.